AF271280

RODEO

By S.L. Hamilton

VISIT US AT WWW.ABDOPUBLISHING.COM

Published by ABDO Publishing Company, 8000 West 78th Street, Suite 310, Edina, MN 55439. Copyright ©2010 by Abdo Consulting Group, Inc. International copyrights reserved in all countries. No part of this book may be reproduced in any form without written permission from the publisher. A&D Xtreme™ is a trademark and logo of ABDO Publishing Company.

Printed in the United States of America, North Mankato, Minnesota.
102009
012010

 PRINTED ON RECYCLED PAPER

Editor: John Hamilton
Graphic Design: John Hamilton
Photos: iStockphoto, p. 2-3, 6 (inset), 6-7, 9 (inset), 18-19, 24-25; John Hamilton, cover, p. 1, 4-5, 8, 9, 10-11, 12 (inset), 12-13, 14-15, 16 (inset), 16-17, 18 (inset), 20-21, 22-23, 24 (inset), 26, 27, 28, 29, 39-31, 32.

Library of Congress Cataloging-in-Publication Data

Hamilton, Sue L., 1959-
  Rodeo / S.L. Hamilton.
     p. cm. -- (Xtreme sports)
  Includes index.
  ISBN 978-1-61613-004-6
  1. Rodeos--Juvenile literature. I. Title.
  GV1834.H36 2010
  791.8'4--dc22
                        2009045276

CONTENTS

XTREME

RODEO

Professional rodeo is a sport with roots in the Old West. To compete and win, cowboy and cowgirl athletes must be agile, tough, and have excellent riding skills.

Xtreme Fact

In timed events, competitors race against the clock and each other. In roughstock events, scores are based on the performance of the rider and the animal.

RODEO

In the days of the Old West in the mid-1800s, ranch hands gathered and competed to see who had the best style when it came to riding untrained horses. When they were on the trail, cowboys often had to rope and tie down sick calves for medical treatment. Both of these activities can be seen in modern rodeos. Today, professional cowboys and cowgirls compete for fame and prizes.

HISTORY

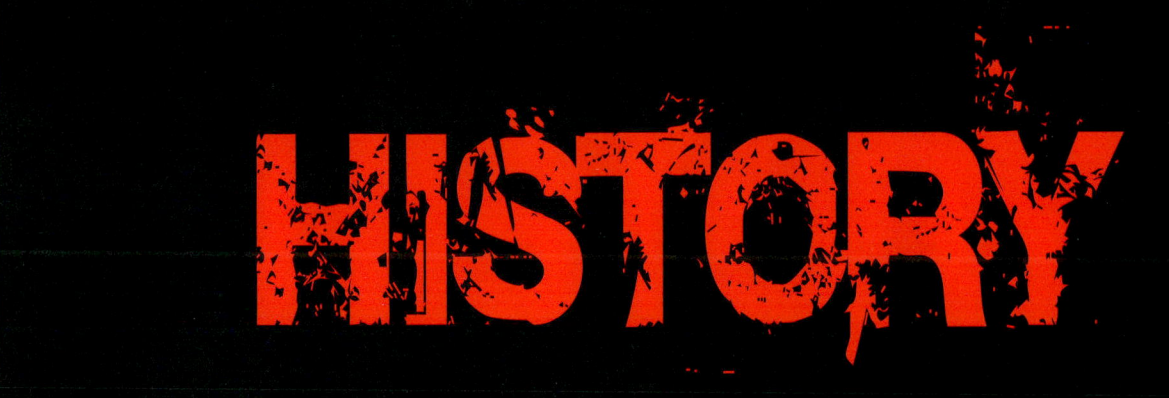

Xtreme Fact

Rodeo is a Spanish word used by early cowboys when they gathered up their cattle. The English translation is "round up."

RODEO

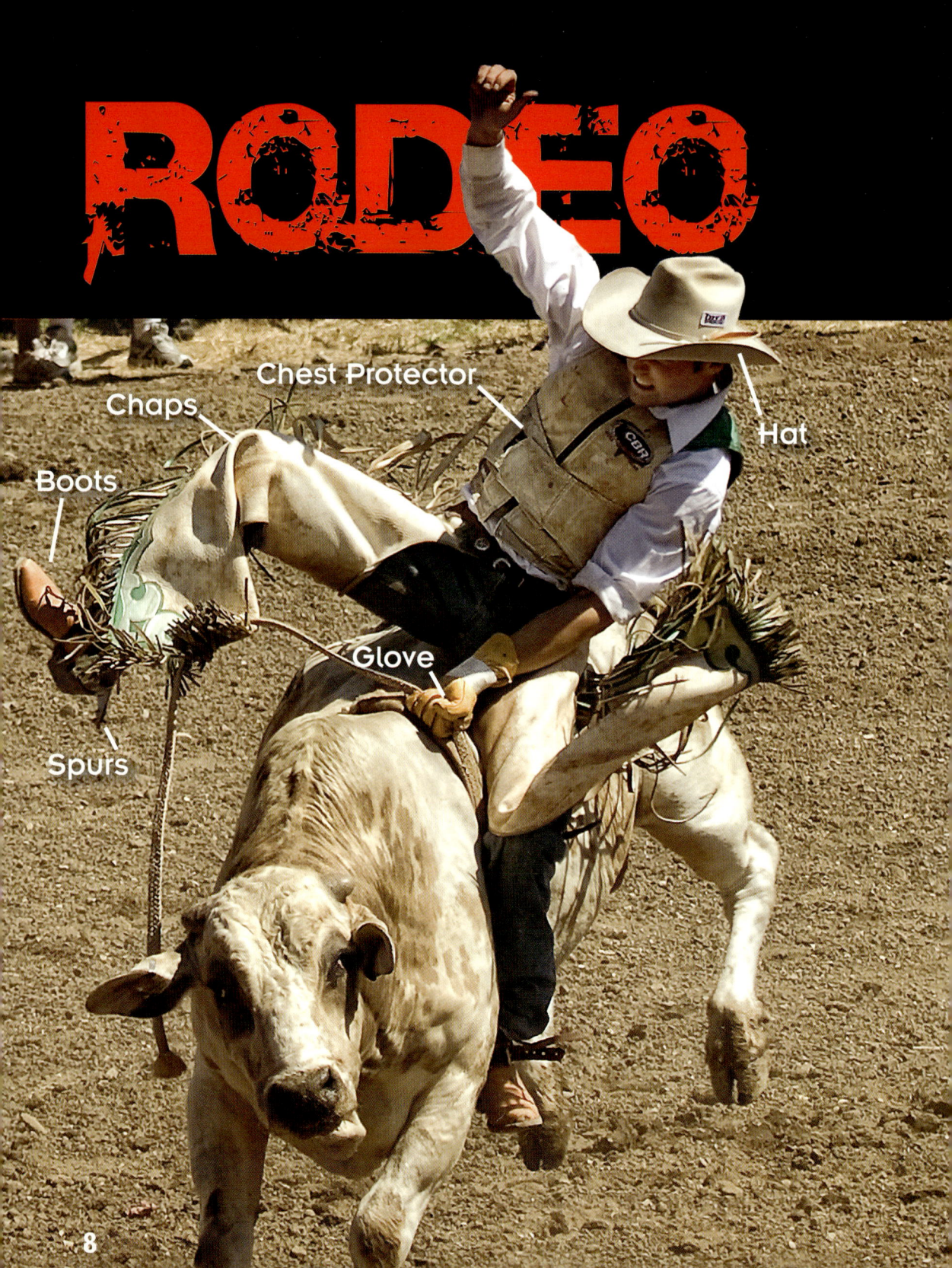

Chaps

Chest Protector

Hat

Boots

Glove

Spurs

EQUIPMENT

Lariat

Horn
Pommel
Seat
Cantle

Strings

Stirrup

Western Saddle

Bridle

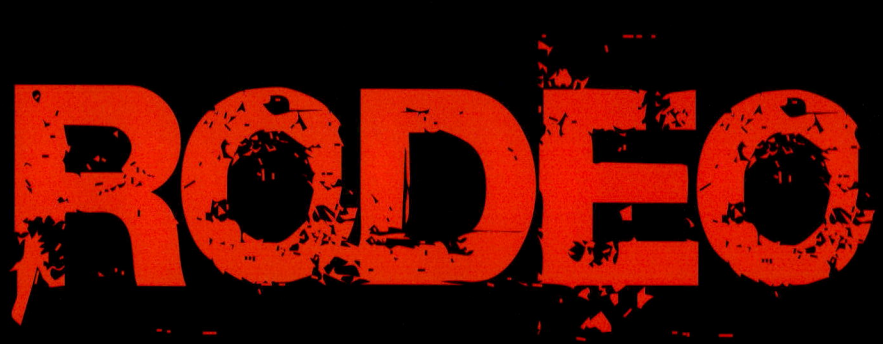

RODEO

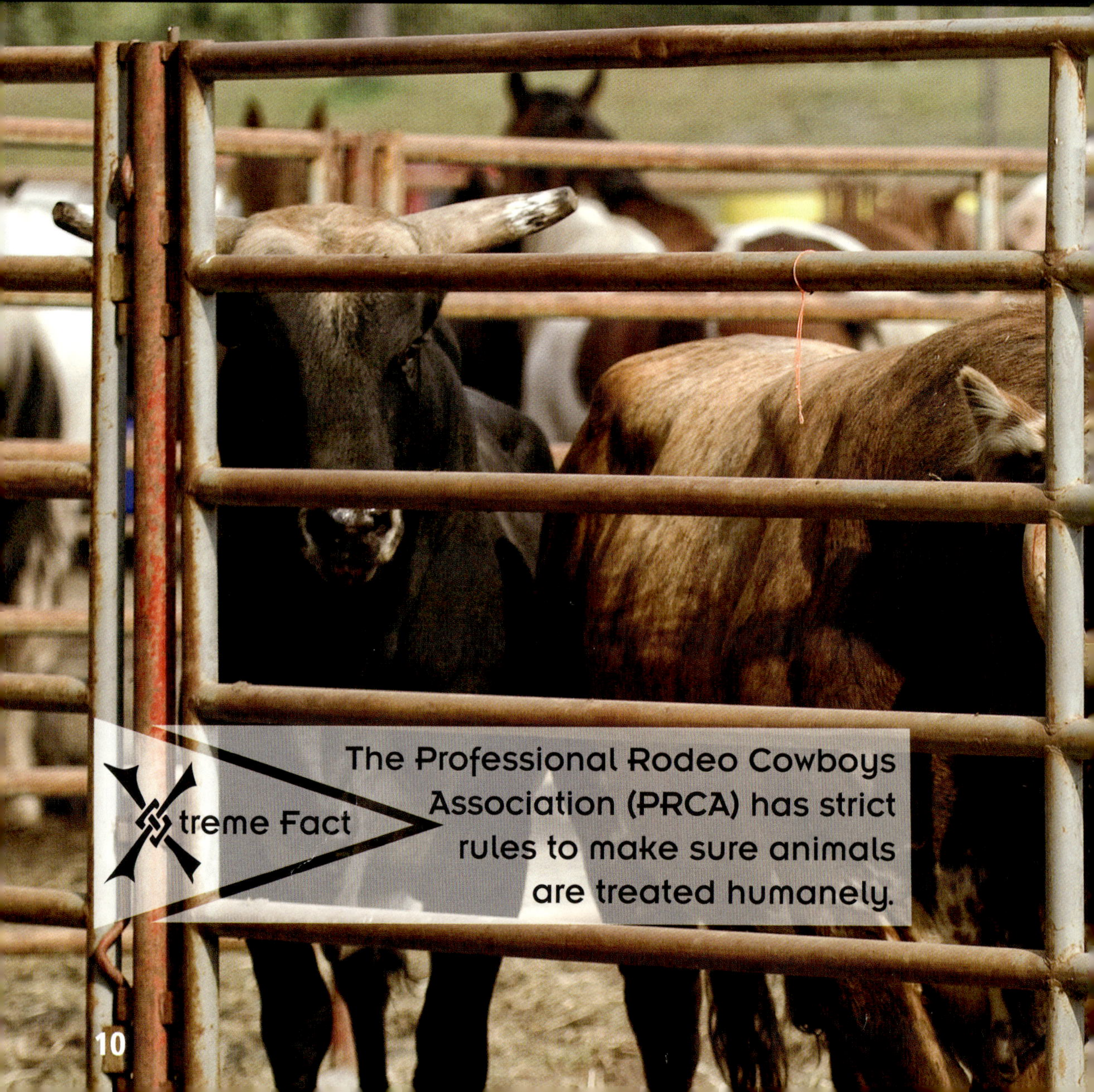

Xtreme Fact

The Professional Rodeo Cowboys Association (PRCA) has strict rules to make sure animals are treated humanely.

LIVESTOCK

Rodeo animals are well cared for. They are a valuable investment to their owners. Livestock injuries are rare, but a veterinarian is always on hand just in case.

Saddle Bronc Riding

Riders try to stay on the bucking horse for eight seconds. They begin with their feet over the bronc's shoulders. If they stay on for the entire ride, they are scored on their balance and control, and how hard the horse bucks. They must not touch the horse or saddle with their free hand.

Bareback Riding

With no saddle and a single handhold called a rigging, riders try to stay on the bucking horse for eight seconds. Bareback riding is a wild event that takes tremendous skill to master.

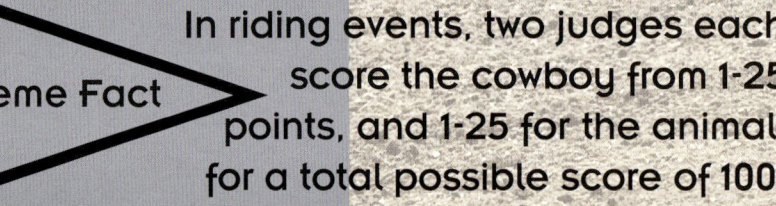

Xtreme Fact

In riding events, two judges each score the cowboy from 1-25 points, and 1-25 for the animal, for a total possible score of 100.

Xtreme Fact Bulls can weigh more than 2,000 pounds (907 kg), but they are extremely quick and agile.

Bull Riding

In rodeo's most dangerous event, riders must stay on a wild, bucking bull for eight seconds. They are allowed to grip a braided rope tied around the bull with just one hand. After the bouncing, twisting bull charges out of the chute, a successful ride requires strong legs and upper body control.

requires precise teamwork between a rider and horse. The calf is given a head start, then the rider gives chase. After roping the calf, the rider dismounts, wrestles the calf to the ground, then ties three legs so the animal cannot get up, just like on working ranches.

Steer Wrestling

Steer wrestling requires as much skill as brute strength. In this timed event, "bulldoggers" slide off their galloping horses at 35 miles per hour (56 kph) onto a steer that weighs about 500 pounds (227 kg). The timer stops when the steer lies flat on its side.

Xtreme Fact

Cowboy Bill Picket may have begun steer wrestling in the early 1900s. Picket is a member of the National Rodeo Hall of Fame.

If the heeler manages to rope only one hind foot, the team is penalized five seconds.

Team Roping

Two cowboys work together in team roping. The first cowboy is called the "header." He ropes the steer by the horns or neck. The second cowboy, the "heeler," then attempts to rope both hind feet. The timer stops when both cowboys' horses face each other. Team roping is a skill used on working ranches.

Barrel Racing

Cowgirls most often compete in this timed event. Riders enter the arena at a full gallop, then race in a cloverleaf pattern around three large barrels. There is a five-second penalty if a barrel is tipped over. Barrel racing requires superb horse-handling skills. Victory can be measured in hundredths of a second.

An electronic trigger starts the timer as the rider enters the arena.

Bareback Riding

Bull Riding

Barrel Racing

Steer Wrestling

RODEO

Rodeo clowns are a very important part of the bull riding event. They are so important, they are often called bullfighters. Their job is to distract the bull and give protection after a rider has been thrown. The bullfighter puts himself in harm's way, getting the mean-tempered bull's attention while allowing the cowboy to scramble to safety. Some bullfighters dress in clown outfits, doing double duty as crowd entertainers.

CLOWNS

Xtreme Fact The "barrel man" can quickly jump in a padded barrel for safety.

Bridle
Headgear used to direct the movement of a horse. A "bit" goes in the horse's mouth, held there by a "headstall" harness made of leather straps. "Reins" are straps attached to the bit that are used by the rider to control the horse.

Bronc
Short for "bronco." A wild or partly tamed horse.

Chaps
Sturdy leg coverings, often made of leather, that buckle over a horse rider's pants and protect against brush or dirt. The word is usually pronounced "shaps."

Chest Protector
A thick, sturdy shield, worn like a vest, that protects a rider from the impact of falling off an animal, or from being kicked or trampled. Many rodeo competitors also choose to wear added protection, such as helmets and mouthguards.

GLOSSARY

Chute

A narrow pen where horses and bulls are held. Riders sit on animals in the chute. When the riders signal they are ready, the pen door is opened, and the animal charges into the arena.

Lariat

A stiff nylon rope, used to snare cattle. The lariat is looped around one end to form a noose called a lasso. Because the rope is stiff, the noose stays open when thrown, but is easily tightened when pulled.

Spur

A metal tool worn on the heel of riding boots. The toothed wheel at the end is called a rowel. In rodeos, rowels are dulled and turn freely. Spurs are not designed to hurt the animal, but to direct it. Horse and bull hide is much thicker than human skin. Saddle bronc and bareback riding competitors are scored partly on the skill of their spurring technique.

INDEX